# GRANNY
## knows best

JOAN BUCKLEY

PORTICO

# CONTENTS

# INTRODUCTION

Welcome to the royal kingdom of grandmothers, Your Granniness! Becoming a granny is a wonderful and exciting event. A new life comes into yours and changes it in many ways: you have the joy of motherhood again but at one remove (and without the sleepless nights) and passing on your wit and wisdom is one of the great pleasures, if not duties, of your role. As the old saying goes, your biscuit tin is as full as your heart and, as the new saying expands, your head is as full as any dictionary, encyclopaedia or household manual.

This book is yours to enjoy and to make use of as you see fit. It is full of all things grandmothers know or need to know and share in order to be the best granny, grandma, nanny, or nana in town.

# Granny Wisdom

# Good Housekeeping

Some people derive great satisfaction from housework done well, some people quite enjoy it and others find it a complete drudge. You clean and tidy, and then you do it all over again (the next day, the next week, the next month ... depending on your regime!).

One thing's for certain, however – despite all the progress in the equality of the sexes, more often than not it still falls to the woman of the house to do the majority of the work. So, by the time you get to be a granny, you'll have vacuumed a million miles of carpet and collected a billion bags of dust mites and crumbs (OK, that's a bit of an exaggeration, but you get the well-polished picture). And the older you get, the faster time goes by and the more it seems as though it was only yesterday that you were vacuuming up the cat hairs, when in reality it was at least a week ago. So if your son-in-law asks if the housework fairies could wash his car, try some of these clean and shiny pearls of wisdom on him.

## Cleanliness is next to godliness.

*As many a child with a dirty face has been told, down through the centuries.*

## You've got to eat a ton of muck afore you die (as they say in Yorkshire – southerners prefer a 'peck of dirt').

*Not if the manufacturers of the endless array of antibacterial gels/ wipes/cleansers etc. can help it.*

*And on a similar note:*
## What won't choke will fatten.

## Clean dirt is no poison.

## Cleaning the house will not pay the rent.

*One for those who only dust in months with a ζ in them.*

# A bit of elbow grease won't do you any harm.

*Looking at the latest complicated gadget (yet another thing to find a place for) that professes to save you time.*

# If each man sweeps before his own door, the whole street is clean.

*A man sweeping the porch? Are you kidding!*

# A new broom sweeps clean, but the old one knows the corners.

*Applies to kitchens (and other workplaces).*

# A pig that is used to wallowing in the mud looks for a clean person to rub against.

*Never was a truer word spoken — and for 'pig' substitute 'cat', 'dog' or even 'grandchild'.*

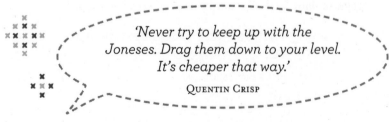

'Never try to keep up with the Joneses. Drag them down to your level. It's cheaper that way.'

Quentin Crisp

**Don't throw out the dirty water until you have the clean water in.**

*Prudent when there's a hosepipe ban.*

**A cat lick and a promise.**

*How you do the cleaning when you've far better things to do.*

**A woman's work is never done.**

*But that doesn't mean you can't help her, guys.*

*And finally, three sayings for those who like to be extremely tidy:*
**A place for everything and everything in its place.**

**Ship-shape and Bristol fashion.**

**A tidy ship is a safe ship.**

*Applies to ships, kitchens, bathrooms, cars, even handbags.*

# PEARLS OF CLEAN WISDOM

'Have nothing in your home that you do not know to be useful or believe to be beautiful.'

WILLIAM MORRIS

'Cleanliness is indeed next to Godliness.'

RABBI PHINEHAS
BEN YAIR

'I think housework is far more tiring and frightening than hunting is, no comparison, and yet after hunting we had eggs for tea and were made to rest for hours, but after housework people expect one to go on just as if nothing special had happened.'

NANCY MITFORD

'Have a place for everything and keep the thing somewhere else; this is not a piece of advice, it is merely a custom.'

MARK TWAIN

'He taught me housekeeping; when I divorce I keep the house.'

ZSA ZSA GABOR

'If you can't be clean, at least be good.'

BARBARA MOSELEY

# Granny Stats

The world's oldest orca has been dubbed 'Granny' unofficially – her 'official' name, given by researchers, is the much more prosaic J2. She is probably over 100 years old – way beyond the 60–80 years that is the usual lifespan for a killer whale. Just what is she on?! Granny is thought to have been born in 1911 – a year before the sinking of the *Titanic*. She is still top dog – or rather matriarch – in charge of her killer whale pod. She helps to rear the young orcas and babysits them while their parents are out at work, hunting! And now for some human grannies...

## OLDEST

Leandra Becerra Lumbreras was born on 31 August 1887 in a small Mexican village. She is thought to be the oldest person ever to have lived and has 20 grandchildren, 73 great-grandchildren and 55 great-great-grandchildren. She cites her secret to longevity as eating well, sleeping lots and never getting married! She was nearly 27 when World War I broke out and a sprightly 81 when Neil Armstrong first set foot on the moon in 1969. No doubt Leandra would have liked to have joined him.

## YOUNGEST

Rifca Stanescu from Romania became a grandmother at just 23. She gave birth at 12 and her daughter gave birth at 11. Her grandson will call her *Bunica* in Romanian (see page 128 for more grannies in translation).

## STRONGEST

A 'granny shot' is a method of shooting a basketball. It is usually looked upon as a weak shot by an unskilled player – implying that grannies are fragile and feeble. Whoever coined this phrase had obviously never heard of Effie Nielsen, who at the age of 90, broke three world records at the State of Nevada's power-lifting and bench-pressing championships. The tiny 105lb grandmother (that's 7½ stone or 47kg, depending upon your unit of choice) hoisted a staggering 135lb (61kg). We should all have what she's having. She's putting the 'Grr' back in Granny!

## MOST AVERAGE!

In the UK, the average age to become a grandparent is just 47 – the average Brit's biological clock must be on fast-forward! Just a century ago we could only expect to live until around 50. In the USA, the average first-time granny clocks in at 48. Do a survey of your own friends, and you may be surprised at what you find.

Granny
Wisdom

# In the Kitchen

**Grandma's kitchen has become something of a cliché – conjuring up images of a wooden table and chairs, stew bubbling on the stove and an apple-cheeked grandmother standing in front of a mixing bowl, wiping her floury hands on her slightly-too-tight apron.**

Stop right there! The reality for many a modern granny is a shiny, stainless-steel kitchen, full of the latest gadgets, a fridge that tells you what you're running short of and a shelf full of TV-chef cookbooks that order you to use foodstuffs you never knew existed. But the basic impression remains the same, even if these days you prefer to spend less time cooking and have a useful supply of frozen ready-meals, but still like to turn out a tempting Sunday roast and a perfect Victoria sponge. And it's lovely to invite all the family round for Stir-up Sunday to mix the Christmas pudding or to make cupcakes with your granddaughter in various shades of pink. There's nothing like the smell of newly baked bread to welcome the grandchildren (and the prospective buyers, so you can get that lovely open-plan kitchen with underfloor heating on your next house move).

'After a good dinner one can forgive anybody, even one's own relations.'

OSCAR WILDE

## If you can't stand the heat, get out of the kitchen.

*I'm happy cooking on my own (with my glass of wine).*

## Too many cooks spoil the broth.

*If Granny's in the kitchen, it's best to leave her to it. Offering to peel potatoes at a reasonable distance is OK and licking the cake mixer bowl with Granny is a special treat.*

## Be an angel in the kitchen and a demon in the bedroom.

*One for other grannies to laugh at.*

## Everything but the kitchen sink.

*What some grannies take with them on holiday.*

## Bubbe says 'eat something!'

*Worries go down better with soup.*
*Chicken, of course — 'Bubbe' is 'grandma' in Yiddish.*

## STRICTLY BAKING

How many times a week do you say the word 'cake' (without indulging in it?). It features in as many sayings as there are colours of icing on a tray of fondant fancies.

**It's a piece of cake.**

**It's selling like hot cakes.**

**You can't have your cake and eat it.**

**That's the icing on the cake.**

**Shut your cake hole.**

*Yorkshire for 'please be quiet'!*

**Let them eat cake.**

*Uttered beneath a powdered wig.*

And if you've had enough of the grandkids, try this old saying on them:

**Go home will yer, ya ma's got cake.**

Cake in moderation, like all things, is good. Baking has become the hobby du jour and satisfies our taste buds, our creative instincts and our TV viewing habits. It's like meditation but with something to eat at the end. Shakespeare got it right in *Twelfth Night*: 'Do you think because you are virtuous, there shall be no more cakes and ale?'

Finally, try and work out what this one means:

**Every cake hath its make; but a scrape cake hath two.**

*Answer on the back of the tin.*

## Not worth crying over spilled milk.

*Just wipe it up. It's not going to harm anyone unless you've spilled it in Grandpa's car, in which case you're in big trouble.*

## If there's an odour, use soda.

*Baking soda gets rid of lots of 'oops' and 'whoops'.*

## Put a banana in with your avo, it will be ripe by the morrow.

*That's avocado. Try it, it works. Use a paper bag.*

## If there's mould on your cheese, cut off an inch if you please.

*Makes rhyme and reason.*

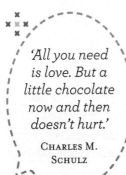

*'All you need is love. But a little chocolate now and then doesn't hurt.'*

CHARLES M.
SCHULZ

## A dash of vinegar makes the sins 'ere go.

*Vinegar cleans up lots of ills 'n' spills (windows, fridge shelves, pans with stains).*

## Laughter is brightest where food is best.

*One from Ireland — not mentioning potatoes, yer mammy or leprechauns, so stereotype-free for a change.*

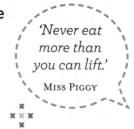

*'Never eat more than you can lift.'*
Miss Piggy

*And from Poland, where they are clearly not watching their waistlines or their weekly alcohol consumption:*

## Fish to taste right must swim three times, in water, butter and in wine.

## The way to a man's heart is through his stomach.

*It's got to be the way to just about everyone else's too, including the cat, the dog and the difficult relation.*

# BUTTER

Long before margarine and low-fat spreads – not to mention good and bad cholesterol – there was butter. Back in the day of the milkmaid in her mob-cap it just came with salt and without, whereas these days it can be churned, loaded with omega-3, whipped, blended, flavoured ... But whatever its current trendy permutations, it's not surprising that a kitchen staple that has been around for so long should feature in a number of wise old sayings.

### Butter wouldn't melt.

*The innocent demeanour of a grandchild who has just done something very naughty. The guilty party may also look like 'the cat who got the cream'.*

### Bread always falls on the buttered side.

*AKA sod's law – when there's a choice of two outcomes, you suddenly get that sinking feeling, knowing the least desirable will prevail.*

*On the other hand, it is always good to ...*

### Know on which side your bread is buttered.

### Fine words butter no parsnips.

*Unlikely to be uttered by anyone not in a television costume drama these days.*

### Butter someone up.

*What you do when you want a cup of tea/the remote control/a lift to your tap-dancing class.*

## ALCOHOL

You need a drink when ... your sponge cake emerges from the oven looking like a biscuit, your grandchild has just been sick on your new pashmina/cardi, or, worst of all, you've just received another of those Christmas round-robin letters full of the exploits of other people's grandchildren – Emily passed all her exams with flying colours a year early, Ethan has had his poem published in the local paper and Savannah has launched a new dotcom and is set to make a fortune. Compare with your offspring's offspring – Alfie has a new bike, Ellie swam two lengths of the pool and Jack got caught smoking an illegal substance at a music festival. But there's many a proverb preaching discretion around the demon drink, so if you feel inclined to reach for a sherry, it might be prudent to remember that:

**He who drinks a little too much drinks too much.**

**Eat at pleasure, drink by measure.**

*Wine is also notorious for loosening the tongue – if you would like to sound lofty in Latin:*

**In vino veritas.**

*Which translates as 'In wine, there's truth'.*

*And a further word or two of caution:*

**When the wine is in, the wit is out.**

*Although equally:*

**The drunk mind speaks the sober heart.**

*And on a similar note, as anyone who has ever had one too many over lunch and found themselves being uncharacteristically frank about a friend's outfit/hair/husband:*

**What soberness conceals, drunkenness reveals.**

*While for making life look rosier through the alcoholic haze of 'beer goggles':*

**Wine is the best broom for troubles.**

**Wine makes old wives wenches.**

*But to level up the playing field in this age of equality: gin makes old guys gorgeous. Hmm, it would take a lot in most cases.*

*In other words:*

**A good drink makes the old young.**

*Which works a treat for both sexes.*

# WINE TALKS

'In wine there is wisdom, in beer there is freedom, in water there is bacteria.'

BENJAMIN FRANKLIN

'I'm like old wine. They don't bring me out very often, but I'm well preserved.'

ROSE KENNEDY, ON HER 100TH BIRTHDAY

'Age is just a number. It's totally irrelevant unless, of course, you happen to be a bottle of wine.'

JOAN COLLINS

'I don't have a drink problem except when I can't get one.'

TOM WAITS

'A hangover is the wrath of grapes.'

DOROTHY PARKER

'Wine improves with age. The older I get, the better I like it.'

ANONYMOUS

'Everybody should believe in something; I believe I'll have another drink.'

UNKNOWN

# The Grandmother of Europe

Queen Victoria married Prince Albert in 1840 and had nine children – four sons and five daughters, including the future King Edward VII and the German Empress, Victoria. Victoria and Albert produced 42 grandchildren and 87 great-grandchildren. Their eldest child, Princess Victoria, married Prince Frederick of Prussia and was mother to the future Emperor Wilhelm II. Queen Victoria was also grandmother to King George V via her son Edward VII. Her children married into the houses of Prussia, Denmark, Russia, Schleswig-Holstein, Waldeck and Battenburg, and the current monarchs of Great Britain, Spain, Sweden, Denmark, Norway and Luxembourg are all her descendants. Imagine reading Queen Victoria's Christmas round-robin letter: 'One's children are doing terribly well on their gap years abroad and it looks as though they will be going into the family business in a number of influential countries ...'

# Granny's Favourite Films

*It's a Wonderful Life* (they don't make films like that anymore)

*The Sound of Music* (or anything with Julie Andrews)

*Singin' in the Rain*

*Nanny McPhee*

*Mrs Doubtfire*

*Thelma and Louise*

*To Kill a Mockingbird*

*E.T.*

*Finding Nemo*

*Toy Story* (1, 2 or 3)

*Harry Potter* (any)

*The Lord of the Rings* series

*Mamma Mia!*

# Love and Marriage

**Love and marriage go together like the proverbial horse and carriage. You start the journey through life hand in hand on the loved-up cart, but you're bound to hit some bumps along the way, stopping at major crossroads and having the odd puncture, so it's important to be ready to negotiate them.**

You've been down that road, got the sore bottom and the T-shirt and are therefore in a good position to pass on your experience to those just starting out on it or at least thinking about it.

We're all human (although some of us may have decided we prefer to live with our pets instead by now) and, de facto, we all have our little foibles and faults. The Japanese have a philosophy that celebrates imperfect beauty known as *wabi-sabi*. This is not to be confused with that really hot green stuff you put on sushi that makes your face go red, but a term deriving from their traditional tea ceremony. It teaches that just as we embrace and accept well-loved teacups with little chips on the tea tray of life, we should all learn to embrace and accept the imperfections in others.

'' 'Tis better to
have loved and lost
than never to have
loved at all.'

ALFRED, LORD
TENNYSON

## Mr (or Ms) Right will find you when you're not looking for him.

*You can look and look and then, just when you have given up looking and are getting on with life, he or she will come along.*

## Love will come knocking when you least expect it.

*One day — maybe on a bad hair day, when you broke your heel running for the bus home — Mr (or indeed Miss) McDream will knock on the door and Cupid will let loose his arrow. Make sure you let them in.*

## You can go through the wood and still come out with a crooked stick.

*Sometimes looking for love is like being in a supermarket and hunting for a tin of caviar among the own-brand sardines, which are, quite frankly, best left on the shelf — not like you. Sometimes you can't see the wood for the trees, but keep looking. You'll find that hidden hoard of happiness soon. Mixing metaphors is generally not advisable but in this case grannies make an exception (see the bit about horses and tea cups, too!).*

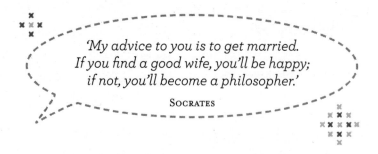

'My advice to you is to get married.
If you find a good wife, you'll be happy;
if not, you'll become a philosopher.'

SOCRATES

## Marrying is easy, housework is hard.

*Just slipped this one in here …*

## Absence makes the heart grow fonder.

*Spending time apart can help you grow closer to loved ones,
stranger-ly enough. But long-distance love can be hard to sustain.
So find a happy medium or a very fast plane.*

## When you go out, always keep your hand on your halfpenny.

*A very old but wise piece of advice: keep money for a taxi
(and your legs crossed)!*

## Treasure friendship.

*If your lover is also your best friend, your relationship really
is on solid ground.*

## Seize the day.

*You can also do it in Latin* (carpe diem) *if the object of your affections sports a toga. But even if he's just in jeans and a T-shirt or slippers and a comfy cardi, don't let the grass grow under your feet — go one better and seize the hour, the moment. If Mr Potentially Right is knocking on the door, don't hide behind the sofa or beneath those silly earphones on your head. Answer it.* Aperiesque ostium! (*Latin for 'open the door'*).

## If not now, then when?

*See above.*

## Love comes in many guises.

*That's not the plural of guys, by the way.*

*But it's cruel to* **lead someone up the garden path** *or* **keep them dangling on the end of a string**. *And* **never marry in haste** *without having taken the time to build up* **a bottom drawer** *or you will surely* **repent at leisure**. *A bad case of* **the seven-year-itch** *is bound to follow, and despite your vows you will both end up being* **put asunder**. *Yay, verily, I say unto you.*

# LOVE LETTERS

'The first to apologise is the bravest. The first to forgive is the strongest. The first to forget is the happiest.'

UNKNOWN

'I have yet to hear a man ask for advice on how to combine marriage and a career.'

GLORIA STEINEM

'A happy marriage is a long conversation which always seems too short.'

ANDRÉ MAUROIS

'There is nothing nobler or more admirable than when two people who see eye-to-eye keep house as man and wife, confounding their enemies and delighting their friends.'

HOMER

'Some people ask the secret of our long marriage. We take time to go to a restaurant two times a week. A little candlelight, dinner, soft music and dancing ... she goes Tuesdays, I go Fridays.'

HENRY YOUNGMAN

'Your task is not to seek for love, but merely to seek and find all the barriers within yourself that you have built against it.'

RUMI

'It is not a lack of love, but a lack of friendship that makes unhappy marriages.'

FRIEDRICH NIETZSCHE

'Chains do not hold a marriage together. It is threads, hundreds of tiny threads which sew people together through the years.'

SIMONE SIGNORET

# In Two Minds

Every woman is entitled to change her mind, but grannies especially so. Just make sure you don't utter any of these sayings in the same breath, or you might sound rather indecisive and a bit dotty.

**You're never too old to learn.**

*But then again:*

**You can't teach an old dog new tricks.**

**Actions speak louder than words.**

*Although, as is also often said:*

**The pen is mightier than the sword.**

**Look before you leap.**

*On the other hand:*

**He who hesitates is lost.**

**The more, the merrier.**

*Depending on who the 'more' are, otherwise:*

**Two's company; three's a crowd.**

**Birds of a feather flock together.**

*But equally:*

**Opposites attract.**

**Don't judge a book by its cover.**

*However, remember that:*

**Clothes maketh the man (or woman).**

**Never look a gift horse in the mouth.**

*But, rather xenophobically, unless a wooden horse is involved:*

**Beware of Greeks bearing gifts.**

**It's better to be safe than sorry.**

*Although it's true that:*

**Nothing ventured, nothing gained.**

**Never put off till tomorrow what you can do today.**

*Although you should:*

**Cross that bridge when you come to it.**

Granny
Wisdom

# Getting on
# with the Family

**'Family first' is one of the earliest pieces of advice we hear and the one we are most likely to remember and pass on.**

It doesn't mean you shouldn't try to help your friends and those outside the immediate family too, but looking after those closest to you is important – charity begins at home, after all. Giving them time, making them a priority, keeping lines of communication open and the peace at family gatherings, are all part of a granny's family toolkit – as are avoiding points of conflict, understanding how they come about if you don't manage to avoid them and just being there to talk to. With today's 'blended' and often long-distance, more complex and extended families, Grandma Diplomacy is needed more than ever. It doesn't come naturally to everyone but it is a powerful concept – even presidents use it. You're good at it because you've seen it all before and you know what can happen when folk fall out. And it ain't pretty. Experience is invaluable and your wisdom from the sidelines or the position of matriarch can be of enormous value to those in the trenches or on the family frontline.

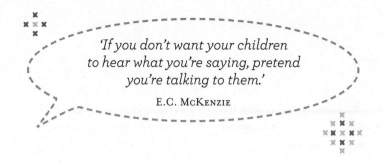

'If you don't want your children
to hear what you're saying, pretend
you're talking to them.'

E.C. McKenzie

## Home is where the heart is.

*It's also where the hearth is. So don't drop your aitches
and you'll be OK.*

## You can choose your friends but you can't choose your family.

*That includes Granny, but yours is, of course, the best.*

## Blood is thicker than water ... and a lot of water flows under the bridge.

*Meaning your family is important no matter what, even if they ask
you to cross a bridge too far. If that's not too confusing.*

## Treat your family like friends and your friends like family.

*This saying goes without saying. And while you're at it, do unto
others as you would have them do unto you. The language may be
a little archaic, but the message is sound.*

## Don't wash (or dry) your dirty linen in public.

*Discretion is key. Nobody wants to know that you've just had a huge fight with your husband. Or see his ancient underwear on the washing line …*

## Never go to bed on an argument.

*Clear the air before you hit the hay if it's a big issue. If it's small, go to sleep and you probably won't remember it the next day.*

*'A grandmother is a mother who has a second chance.'*

UNKNOWN

One of life's greatest mysteries is how the boy who wasn't good enough to marry your daughter can be the father of the smartest grandchild in the world.

*This is called son-in-law's revenge.*

## Charity begins at home.

*So do most arguments, but that's another matter.*

## Do not wear out your welcome.

*If your daughter-in-law has put her pyjamas on, it's time to head for the door.*

## Guests, like fish, go off after three days.

*See above.*

## Love thy neighbour, but do not pull down thy hedge.

*Or the boundary wall … but watch the height of your Leylandii.*

## The family that eats together, stays together.

*So no more eating in different rooms watching different screens.*

## Families are like wardrobes: they are full of things that keep you warm and the odd skeleton.

*And some things that are now vintage and valuable!*

# RELATIVELY SPEAKING

'The advantage of growing up with siblings is that you become very good at fractions.'

ROBERT BRAULT

'After a good dinner one can forgive anybody, even one's own relations.'

OSCAR WILDE

The reason grandparents and grandchildren get along so well is that they have a common enemy.'

SAM LEVENSON

'Sister is probably the most competitive relationship within the family, but once the sisters are grown, it becomes the strongest relationship.'

MARGARET MEAD

'All happy families are alike; each unhappy family is unhappy in its own way.'

LEO TOLSTOY

'I wish I had the energy that my grandchildren have — if only for self-defence.'

GENE PERRET

'Home is the place where, when you have to go there, they have to take you in.'

ROBERT FROST

# How to Speak Granny

Some sayings are so obscure, they need deciphering. These translations might help!

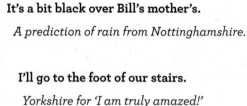

**It's a bit black over Bill's mother's.**

*A prediction of rain from Nottinghamshire.*

**I'll go to the foot of our stairs.**

*Yorkshire for 'I am truly amazed!'*

**Stew the dish rag.**

*What a US Midwesterner might say when putting on a great feast for unexpected guests.*

**Sitting like Piffy on a rock bun.**

*A Mancunian way of describing someone left out or hanging around pointlessly in this descriptive – if opaque – fashion.*

**Don't put your puddings out for breakfast.**

*In other words, don't show off. To which the reply might be, 'The same to you with knobs on' (i.e. right back at yer)!*

**I'll be waiting till Dick docks and he hasn't got a boat.**

*What they say in Liverpool when something may take a long time.*

**Lend us your hat, we're having soup.**

*As one Liverpudlian might say to another, when taking a dim view of someone's poor table manners.*

**She's got a few kangaroos loose in the top paddock.**

*Australian for someone who is losing their marbles … to explain a saying with another saying.*

**I'm as old as me nose and a little bit older than me teeth.**

*A cryptic answer for when some nosy parker asks a granny her age.*

**'Ear all, see all, say nowt. Eat all, sup all, pay nowt. And if ever thou does owt fer nowt – allus do it fer thissen.**

*Yes, that is English. Sort of. This is from Yorkshire and translates as: 'Hear all, see all, say nothing. Eat all, drink all, pay nothing. And if you ever do something for nothing – make sure you do it for yourself.'*

# New Granny Guide

It's time to read the handwriting on the wall. And pretty soon it might be because the grandchildren have got hold of your lipstick and eyeliner and are trying their hand at some Banksy-style art, without the price tag. You're a granny. You have a grandchild. One minute you were feeling proud about having done a reasonably good job as a mother and admiring your all-grown-up child, and then suddenly you've moved up a rank to grandmother. And did anyone ask your permission? It might take some getting used to, but a fact's a fact: 60 may be the new 50, and 80 the new 70, but when your child has a child, you have a grandchild, which means – ready or not – you're a grandmother. But don't panic, it's going to be great! And Grandpa (you'll have to get used to hearing that word too) will be just as discombobulated at first, so you can come to terms with it together.

Just think of all the advantages – you get all the fun without too much of the fuss or the foul. Lots of the happy with less of the nappy, lots of cuddles and not too many puddles. You can be indulgent, spoil them rotten and then drop them off back home, just when they're about to get tired and grumpy (and before you do too). Take your time and read these top tips to being a super granny (show them to Grandpa too – the sporting references will help him understand):

## 1. Be prepared to be flexible and fit in around the parents' regime and wishes

You're in a support role now.

## 2. Respect boundaries

You're not the mum so you don't set the rules. You're on the reserve bench not the pitch.

## 3. Listen and learn

Sometimes it's tricky not to speak up, but keep your mind and ears open and your mouth closed. You've played in the first team but you are wearing the granny shirt now.

# Granny Wisdom

# Good Manners

**It's tempting to look back (through those rose-coloured glasses) and think 'fings ain't what they used t'be'. It's a natural part of getting older and applies to many areas of life, but for some grannies, today's lack of manners is one of the worst offenders.**

Do you feel that modern parents are failing to teach their children the basics of politeness? Thank-you letters seem to be a thing of the past – as many a granny knows, whose grandchild has been dragged to the phone under duress to utter an ungracious word in thanks for a present you chose with care but they can't remember. Even a text or email would be preferable. You can't expect things to be exactly the same as they were in your day, but good manners cost nothing, so it's worth investing in some behaviour shares and giving them to your grandkids as a legacy.

## Manners makyth man.

*The motto of Winchester College, founded by William of Wykeham, can be used as is or with the name of whoever is being chastised in place of the word 'man'. Or:*

## Manners maketh Manners.

*Perfect when Manners is the surname in question.*

## Other times, other manners.

*This doesn't always mean that manners have deteriorated; they may just have morphed with modernity. Or not.*

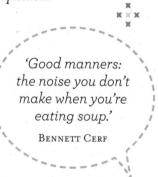

'Good manners: the noise you don't make when you're eating soup.'

BENNETT CERF

## When in Rome, do as the Romans do.

*So when at Grandma's, don't run around the house screaming and yelling at the top of your voice … unless you've seen Grandma doing it, that is.*

## Mind your Ps and Qs.

*Nobody knows what P and Q stand for. 'Please and thank you' will do as an explanation to a five-year-old though, so go with that. 'Platitudes and querulousness' works for the older children.*

## Meat is much, but manners is better.

*Carnivores are less polite than vegetarians. Huh?*

## Poverty is an enemy to good manners.

*But so is too much sugar and too many fizzy drinks.*

## Don't teach your grandmother to suck eggs.

*This saying is as old as the hills, but nobody has a clue where it comes from. After all, why would you want to?*

## A goody two-shoes.

*They were annoying when you were little and now you wish your grandchild were one.*

## Courtesy costs nothing, but good manners even less.

*In supermarket-speak that's 'buy one get one free'.*

58

# RIGHT AND WRONG

And while you're at it, you might as well wade in with a few sayings on the most basic of basics – what's right and wrong. The following may sound rather biblical, but there's nothing wrong with that. A little fire and brimstone will only serve to drive home the message. You may wish to don a false beard and grab a staff – just think Charlton Heston as Moses or Ian McKellen as Gandalf.

The wages of sin is death.

Two wrongs do not make a right.

Give a thief enough rope and he'll hang himself.

Never do evil that good may come of it.

The greater the sinner, the greater the saint.

He who sups with the devil should have a long spoon.

They that sow the wind shall reap the whirlwind.

# A MANNER OF SPEAKING

'Punctuality
is the virtue of
the bored.'

EVELYN WAUGH

'Politeness is only
one half good manners
and the other half
good lying.'

MARY WILSON LITTLE

'Respect for
ourselves guides
our morals; respect
for others guides
our manners.'

LAURENCE STERN

'The hardest job kids face
today is learning good manners
without seeing any.'

FRED ASTAIRE

'Truly good manners are invisible: they ease the way for others, without drawing attention to themselves.'

LYNNE TRUSS

'The test of good manners is to be patient with the bad ones.'

SOLOMON IBN GABIROL

'A man's manners are a mirror in which he shows his portrait.'

JOHANN WOLFGANG VON GOETHE

'Better never than late.'

GEORGE BERNARD SHAW

# Grannies by the Book

During your bedtime-story reading duties ('Can you read that one again, Granny?'), you'll meet yourself in various forms when you discover fictional grannies on the pages of children's books.

The baddest grandmother of all turns out to be a wolf in granny's clothing and not human at all – a hairy, scary creature masquerading as Little Red Riding Hood's grandma, in the eponymous tale. And the moral of this story is, steer clear of grandmothers with big teeth, wet noses and large, hirsute ears. An apple a day is not always the best advice, clearly.

Grandma Josephine in Roald Dahl's *Charlie and the Chocolate Factory* famously said 'I haven't been out of this bed in twenty years and I'm not getting out now for anybody' (a tempting idea) and Grandma Cranky in Dahl's *George's Marvellous Medicine* is mean and frightening, always criticising him and treating him badly. On the other hand, Granny Weatherwax in Terry Pratchett's *Discworld* series is a hard-working and very powerful witch with an unreliable broom and a mistrust of stories, who defends her country against supernatural powers. Or you might identify with Gangsta Granny, the international jewel thief disguised as a boring grandmother, who wears Eau de Cabbage by David Walliams (that's the author of the book, not the creator of the scent ...).

# Granny Mashup

Try as they might to be coherent, grannies sometimes get their sayings mixed up.

Burn that bridge when you get to it.

Don't put all your eggs in one basket or you'll miss the boat.

A bird in the hand catches the worm.

Don't skate on thin ice or the watched pot won't boil.

When the going gets tough, join them.

If you can't stand the heat, don't throw stones.

There's no such thing as a free silver lining.

If you can't beat 'em, get out of the kitchen.

Don't count your chickens until the grass is always greener.

It's no use crying until the fat lady sings.

The apple doesn't fall far from the rolling stone.

Granny
Wisdom

# Mind your Language

**You like to think you're quite easy-going, although perhaps not on the subject of grammar and punctuation. Does the sight of a misplaced apostrophe set your teeth on edge?**

Don't forget that kids these days type everything on a keyboard, even letters to Santa Claus, and all that txtng is bound to have had a detrimental effect on speling ... Never mind. Smiley face. Hashtag. Lol! But it's a grammar minefield out there, so unless you've brushed up on your Shakespeare recently, always think twice before giving advice, particularly if worded as follows:

Don't use commas, that are not needed.

And don't start a sentence with a conjunction.

And while you're at it, it won't create a good impression if you use contractions in formal writing.

Cherish the apostrophe, its often used when not needed, while it's correct use is a thing of beauty.

Be care-ful not to use un-necessary hyphens.

And never use no double negatives.

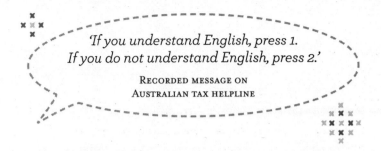

Avoid mixed metaphors and don't count your bulls in a china shop until they've hatched.

Be careful to never split an infinitive.

Always check your emails for spelling mistaks and to be you haven't left any words out.

Always avoid the overuse of exclamation marks!!!

DON'T USE CAPITAL LETTERS – IT LOOKS LIKE YOU'RE SHOUTING.

And one question mark is fine. Otherwise it looks like you're drunk in charge of a keypad. Are you???????????????????

Try not to use too many emoticons. One is fine. Several makes you look sad :0  :P  :(

And last but not least, don't touch clichés with a barge pole.

# ANNOYING YOUTH SPEAK

Some of these may sound familiar:

**Grandchild:** Can I get a (latest toy) for my birthday?

**You (through pursed lips):** Please may I have a (latest toy) for my birthday.

**You:** How are you today?

**Grandchild:** Good.

**You:** Not good. 'Very well', or 'Fine, thank you'.

**Grandchild:** Whatever.

**Grandchild:** Me and Jeffrey ...

**You (through gritted teeth):** 'Jeffrey and I ...' carry on.

**Grandchild to waitress:** Can I get a milkshake?

**You:** Please could I have a milkshake.

**Grandchild to waitress:** Can we get two milkshakes?

**Teen grandchild:** It's like, well, like, sooo cool of you to like, like my friends, Gran.

Silence.

**Grandchild:** Granny, Henry (elder brother) keeps saying he's bare hench.

**You:** You mean Bear Grylls?

**Grandchild:** Bare girls? That's like so rude, Gran.

And if you want to nail yooftalk 110 per cent:

**Stroppy grandteen:** Granny, could I have a lift to the game?

**You:** Yeh, like that's gonna happen? I'm hanging out with Grandpa in our crib in our own manor. It's going to be sick!*

(*I am afraid I can't. Grandpa and I are staying in today and having a lovely afternoon together.)

'Waiting for the German verb is surely the ultimate thrill.'

FLANN O'BRIEN

*'This is the sort of bloody nonsense up with which I will not put!'*

WINSTON CHURCHILL, CHANNELLING YODA, ON THE ENDING OF A SENTENCE WITH A PREPOSITION

'Good intentions are invariably ungrammatical.'

ATTRIBUTED TO OSCAR WILDE

'What really alarms me about President Bush's "War on Terrorism" is the grammar. How do you wage war on an abstract noun? How is "Terrorism" going to surrender? It's well known, in philological circles, that it's very hard for abstract nouns to surrender.'

TERRY JONES

'A synonym is a word you use when you can't spell the other one.'

BALTASAR GRACIÁN

'Sticklers unite, you have nothing to lose but your sense of proportion, and arguably you didn't have a lot of that to begin with.'

LYNNE TRUSS

# Granny Dos

It's your role to support and encourage. Remember to give new parents time and space. Grannies are at one remove when grandchildren first arrive and should wait for a signal to get more hands-on. Pass on your wisdom sparingly as and when it is asked for, particularly to a DILAMOYG (daughter-in-law and mother of your grandchildren). But maybe keep this term to yourself ...

Praise the parents on their wonderful parenting, their beautiful and talented if not precociously bright child and delightful choice of name.

Sprinkle your conversation liberally with any of the following:

**What a beautiful baby.**

**What a lovely colour for a pram/nursery/car seat!**

**She has your gorgeous smile and bright eyes.**

**He is obviously going to be clever like his mother/father.**

**She is so advanced for her age.**

**He is going to break hearts.**

**Is she walking/talking/smiling already?**

**You look slimmer than before you were pregnant.**

*The most dazzling of white lies.*

**I am the proudest/luckiest/happiest granny in the world.**

*But hopefully no white lies involved here.*

**All my friends are jealous of my beautiful grandchild.**

*And tell me they aren't old enough to be grandparents yet...*

**The day my first/second/third/grandchild was born was the happiest day of my life.**

*To each of your children when they have children.*

# Granny Don'ts

As the old adage goes, if you can't think of anything nice to say, don't say anything at all. Some things should simply never be said by grannies in family situations. So take your own advice and 'think before you speak'. If any of the following words pop into your head, don't let them pop out of your mouth until you have run them past the 'Foot in Mouth' test.

*On the naming of a grandchild:*

**You're going to call him Mowgli/Mungo/Mandarin/Manhattan? Isn't that a cartoon character/dog/fruit/the name of a New York suburb?**

*At a family get-together where it's a bit noisy:*

**In my day children were seen and not heard.**

*On the state of the house (accompanied by a sweeping look around a room or – an absolute no-no – a finger drawn across a dusty table):*

**It must be so hard keeping the house clean when you both work such long hours.**

*And to the new mother (daughter or daughter-in-law), refrain from any of the following:*

**Have you tried to lose that extra weight yet?**

**I was back at my pre-baby birth weight in three months.**

**This feeding on demand idea is ridiculous. You'll create a rod for your own back.**

**If you relax, baby will too.**

**It's so much easier being a mother today.**

**You all have so much more help nowadays than we did.**

**They all look the same at birth – ugly little things.**

**Are you feeding him/her again?**

**Don't you think he/she should be walking/talking/reading/writing/bilingual by now?**

**Why don't you apply to have one of those TV makeovers/join a slimming club/have liposuction? It would make you feel so much better.**

**You know me, I'm not one to interfere, but ...**

*This last preamble should set off an alarm as soon as it pops into your head, and a big 'STOP' sign should appear. Such words should never be spoken in family situations.*

*And never say to a teenager:*

**Have you put on weight?**

**Looks aren't everything.**

**Why are you wearing that baseball cap back to front?**

**Which one are you again?**

# Granny's Guide to Social Media

Sometimes grannies learn valuable lessons from their peers – grannies do know best, after all. Here are a few tips to bear in mind and dispense to other 21st-century grandparents.

Keep up with the trends in social media, but don't get *too* trendy. It's great that you're online – that you can Skype your grandkids across the street/town/country/world, that you have your own Facebook page and check in regularly at the café/library/bingo or tennis club/gym/airport, but getting too involved with your grandchildren's online lives is like turning up at their parties and sitting in a chair with your camera taking 'lovely snaps for your album'.

Writing on your grandchildren's Facebook page is a complete no-no. There's a fine line between keeping your hand in and sticking your oar in. It's great if they want to 'friend' you and share photos, and you can 'like' some of the posts (i.e. click on a box to confirm that you think what they have written is interesting), but if you see a picture of your granddaughter wearing the flimsiest of clothes on a chilly night DO NOT post a comment on her wall (write a message on their Facebook page) such as:

**Does your mother know you're wearing that?**

**Isn't that your sister's new top?**

**Shouldn't you have a coat on?**

**You should keep your kidneys warm, darling.**

Be smart with your smartphone and on the button online. Technology can be your friend but don't make it your spy. You could lose all your new 'friends' rather quickly.

And make sure you get the names and terms right – you don't want to look a right twitter. You use posts on Facebook; you upload to YouTube and Instagram (a photo- and video-sharing social networking service); you download from the net (aka the Internet or World Wide Web); you Skype friends; you attach photos to an email; and finally, you tweet and use hashtags on Twitter. Just don't embed your friends or upload your twits! Nothing ages you more than malapropisms in techno-speak. If you tell someone the name of a website, you can drop the 'www.' (double-u, double-u, double-u, dot) bit. It ages you and takes an age.

Granny
Wisdom

# Looking after the Pennies

**The getting of and holding on to filthy lucre has been one of our principal preoccupations since Fred Flintstone carved his first stone cheque and Wilma hit the sales at Rocks 'R' Us with her new credit pebble.**

If only they'd had contactless paying in the Stone Age, it would have made wallets and purses a whole lot lighter (you'll be getting to grips with the contactless concept soon if you haven't already – it's not as lonely as it sounds).

Having lived through boom and bust several times, 21st-century grannies are well known for their thrifty ways, championing make-do-and-mend in today's wasteful, throwaway, live-for-today, buy-now-pay-later, bling-bling-kerching society (delete as appropriate – we all have different views). And of course the best things in life are free. When passing on your wi$dom, resist the temptation to sound too critical or 'in my day' about it or you'll risk landing on deaf ears, rolling eyes and the 'yeah, yeah, whatevs' (the mantra of yoof – it would make a good name for a pop group …).

*'A fool and her money are soon courted.'*

Helen Rowland

## Some advice at fourpence is a groat too dear.

*Coined (get it?) in the days when a groat equalled four English pennies. Doesn't apply to advice in Granny's book though.*

## Industry is Fortune's right hand, and Frugality her left.

*And you've only got one pair of hands, as you keep having to tell people.*

### GLOSSARY

There are so many terms for money nowadays. Stay on the money in money matters by pocketing some of these alternatives, but use them parsimoniously:

| | | |
|---|---|---|
| Wonga | Dough | Wedge |
| Moola | Dosh | Sponduliks |
| Kerching | Loot | Smackers |
| Bread | Shekels | Quids |

## When a habit begins to cost money, it's called a hobby.

*Applies to many vices.*

## Ill got, ill spent.

*The opposite of I'll get, I'll spend …*

## A friend you have to buy; enemies you get for nothing.

*So the best things in life aren't free, after all?*

## If the rich could hire someone else to die for them, the poor would make a wonderful living.

*Taking the concept of hired help to extremes.*

## If you pay peanuts, you get monkeys.

*So what do you get if you pay monkey nuts?*

> *'I made my money the old-fashioned way. I was very nice to a wealthy relative right before he died.'*
> MALCOLM FORBES

## Where there's muck there's brass.

*Those Northern folk know their stuff.*

*And in the same vein:*
## Money, like manure, does no good until it's spread.

## Money doesn't grow on trees.

*Clearly not, but a useful phrase for informing your grandchildren that nor do the latest smartphones.*

## Don't spoil the ship for a ha'porth of tar.

*A 'ha'porth' couldn't have bought much tar when this proverb was first coined. Today, you'd probably get a spoonful — and ships are built of steel anyway.*

## Early to bed and early to rise makes you healthy, wealthy and wise.

*So go to bed now as Grandpa and I are tired.*

## You can't take it with you.

*Known as SKI, or spending the kids' inheritance — go on, book that cruise!*

# MONEY TALKS

'An investment in knowledge pays the best interest.'

BENJAMIN FRANKLIN

'There is nothing wrong with a woman welcoming all men's advances as long as they are in cash.'

ZSA ZSA GABOR

'Wealth consists not in having great possessions, but in having few wants.'

EPICTETUS

'A bank is a place that will lend you money if you can prove that you don't need it.'

BOB HOPE

'If you're given a choice between money and sex appeal, take the money. As you get older, the money will become your sex appeal.'

KATHERINE HEPBURN

'Money is the best deodorant.'

ELIZABETH TAYLOR

'Never spend your money before you have it.'

THOMAS JEFFERSON

'If only God would give me some clear sign, like making a large deposit in my name at a Swiss bank.'

WOODY ALLEN

'A bargain is something you can't use at a price you can't resist.'

FRANKLIN JONES

# What Kind of Granny Are You?

**Grannies come in all kinds of shapes, sizes and styles. There's no One-Size-Granny-Fits-All. Just as you don't really know how you're going to feel about being a grandmother until you become one, you can't be sure of what sort you'll turn out to be until you've had a go.**

**The following might offer some useful insights.**

## HANDS-ON OR HANDS-OFF?

Some grannies are the 'HANDS DIRTY' type – literally. They don't mind doing it all over again. They do the nuts and bolts of grandparenting: dirty nappies, snotty noses, projectile vomit, nits, emergency pick-ups, bath-time tantrums, endless bedtime stories, wrinkle-inducing early mornings, loooong weekends and endless school holidays.

Others are rather more MANICURED-HANDS-OFF and feel that having done their job of producing the parent of the child, their role is simply to pop in and out of the grandparenting business as and when their activity-packed and newly liberated lives allow. They are just there for the good times and the photo opportunities at celebrations and parties and those 'you don't look old enough to have a grandchild' moments in the sun.

## ANCIENT OR MODERN?

**GO-GET-'EM GRANNIES** are active, energetic and fun. They go get the kids and take 'em to judo, karate, galleries, museums, swimming, wall-climbing, mountain-biking, gigs, concerts and festivals. They are a Pandora's box of activities and experiences. You may be a crossover 'Glam-ma' too – hip, fashionable, youthful in outlook and appearance. Granddaughters will adore you and ask you to go on double dates when they're older. They will ask to borrow your vintage clothes. Your grandchildren keep you young and fit, and you want to be an active part of their lives for as long as you and your knees are able. You know in your heart that you can be a bit exhausting, but heck, life is for living ...

Or will you be a **'JUST-LIKE-YOUR-OWN-MOTHER' GRANNY**? A bit old-fashioned, a tea-and-TV granny who has the little ones round for something wholesome to eat before early bed after a cuddle on the sofa, a bit of (suitable) TV and a glass of warm milk. You keep time spent together calm and predictable. Routine is key. You know that things have moved on in the world of parenting since your mother looked after your children, but there's no harm in keeping things simple when you're in charge. You're a safe pair of hands. You know what to do in a crisis and with a full nappy. You want to be – and indeed you are – a dependable granny.

## GUNG-HO GRANNIES

Some grannies are **'A CAUTION'**. They are just on the wrong side of fun – they are dangerous. They don't take precautions and have never really grown up (why start now?). They introduce children to a world of edgy excitement well before they should and seriously well before their parents want them to. They deliver them back home, all revved up and impossible to control, waltzing off to their next party/club/tattoo parlour with a 'Ciao, guys, that was fun!', leaving the parents to deal with the aftermath. 'Granny says it's fine' to go to a gig on your own at 13, move out at 15, get a tattoo and piercing before you start secondary school, miss school for a festival 200 miles away. If you think this could be you, think carefully about what the implications are for your relationship with both the parents and the grandchildren.

## LONG-DISTANCE GRANNIES

Grannies whose children live in foreign countries – sometimes at the other end of the world – are the new generation **'SKYPE GRANNIES.'** Generation G. They chat regularly with their children online and keep up with their activities, managing to be a strong presence in their lives despite the distance. Skyping with a webcam becomes an event for all to look forward to, allowing all the family to take part in events and celebrations 'virtually'.

# Fashion

In the '60s and '70s, many a contemporary boomer granny was admonished for the length of her skirt (whether it was a mini – 'it's nothing but a pelmet!' or a maxi – 'it makes you look like a granny, but at least you're decent'; spookily prescient, had you known it at the time) and amount of make-up (pale lipstick, panda eyes, killer nails).

So pot, kettle and black definitely spring to mind for any boomer grannies thinking about admonishing their grandchildren on points of dress. If you're a Glam-ma you will probably be lending your vintage clothing to your granddaughter anyway and advising on make-up. It's not your job to tell the grandchildren 'you're not going out wearing that' (leave that to their parents or you might feel a bit of a hypocrite), but you can offer the benefit of your wisdom and style advice, and hope that some of it rubs off. You could always show them photographs of your own fashion choices at their age …

> 'The odds of going to the store
> for a loaf of bread and coming out with only
> a loaf of bread are three billion to one.'
> Erma Bombeck

## Wear clean underwear every day.

*In case you're hit by a car or a bus! You don't want the doctors and nurses grimacing at your grey Bridget Joneses or Calvin Kleins.*

## You look like you've been dragged through a hedge backwards.

*Uttered by many a granny to their grandsons in their grunge phase (that's the grandsons in their grunge phase, not the grannies).*

## You cannot tell from a man's clothes how much he is making, but you must look at his wife's.

*Less likely to be quoted these days, though there may be a grain of truth in it for couples with a joint bank account. Otherwise this belongs to the days when women were confined to the home.*

## Take your coat off, or you'll not feel the benefit when you go back out (onto Ilkley Moor bah't 'at).

*Those Northerners again. They'll be saying 'always keep your kidneys warm' next ...*

## Mutton dressed as lamb.

*When you optimistically try on something a bit too trendy in a shop, look in the mirror and suddenly there's Bette Davis in* Whatever Happened to Baby Jane? *staring back at you.*

## Keep both legs in one stocking.

*Then things won't go too far, including the wearer.*

## Hang on to it, it's bound to come round again.

*As any fashionista granny knows, with a wardrobe full of clothes from her youth that are now desirable retro pieces. Can't get into them anymore and you'd look ridiculous now anyway? Hold a garage sale and flog them to your granddaughters.*

## Good clothes open all doors.

*And first impressions count.*

## The child will grow, his clothes will not.

*As any granny knows who remembers packing off her own children in clothes with 'plenty of room to grow' on the first day of term.*

# It's snowing down south.

*In other words, your slip is showing. This clearly implies all petticoats are — or rather were — white. Now mostly consigned to the vintage store, some grannies still swear by them as a valuable extra layer on a chilly day and an anti-static barrier betwixt stockings and skirt. For a modern equivalent, see the thong protruding above the jeans. You might like to coin your own phrase for such instances: 'being too wise above your thighs can cause a few too many eyes to rise'.*

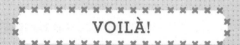

## VOILÀ!

An international wardrobe of fashion sayings – entertaining if sometimes baffling.

**It is good to hold the clothes of one who is swimming. (Italy)**

*Why?*

**He who dresses in others' clothes will be undressed on the highway. (Spain)**

*Que?*

**A woman who wants a child doesn't sleep in her clothes. (Africa)**

*Well! At least it's practical.*

**He who goes to the blacksmith's shop comes home with scorched clothes. (Afghanistan)**

*One to remember next time you visit your local forge.*

# CUT FROM THE SAME CLOTH

'When in doubt, wear red.'

BILL BLASS

'Give a girl the right shoes and she can conquer the world.'

MARILYN MONROE

'If you wear a short enough skirt, the party will come to you.'

DOROTHY PARKER

'I'll stop wearing black when they make a darker colour.'

WEDNESDAY ADDAMS

'Let us give thanks for the invention of spanx.'
UNKNOWN

'And now, I'm just trying to change the world, one sequin at a time.'
LADY GAGA

'I have an iron deficiency. You can tell by how wrinkled my clothes are.'
JAROD KINTZ

'Fashion changes, but style endures.'
COCO CHANEL

'Trendy is the last stage before tacky.'
KARL LAGERFELD

# GRANNY'S T-SHIRT WARDROBE

IF MUMMY
SAYS NO,
ASK GRANNY

GRANNY
KNOWS BEST

SHE'S HAD
LOTS OF TIME
TO PRACTISE

WHEN I GROW
UP, I WANT TO
BE JUST LIKE
GRANDMA

GRANNIES ARE
LIKE OWLS,
THEY HAVE
360-DEGREE
VISION

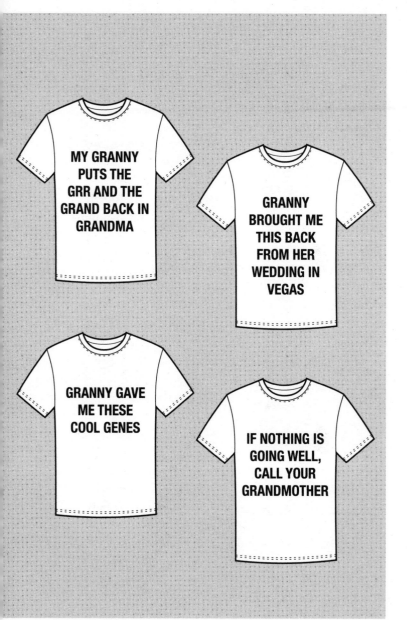

# HAIR

Today's grannies have lived through pretty much every kind of hairstyle – from the peek-a-boo bang and updo, to the backcombed beehive and pixie cut, via the perm, bob, punk Mohawk – OK, maybe not the Mohawk – but as everyone knows, whatever your hairstyle, any day can be a bad hair day. So it's not surprising that it's found its way into a saying or two.

### Long hair and short wit.

*More hair than sense on one's shoulders, as the Hungarians or Russians originally said.*

### Make his hair grow through his hood.

*To cuckold, not a word you hear much nowadays!*

### Keep your hair on.

*Used to calm someone down, whether wearing a wig or not.*

### That will put hairs on your chest.

*Metaphorically speaking only for women, many of whom already have to grapple with enough unwanted hair on their body.*

### Hair of the dog.

From the days when people thought you could ward off rabies by putting hair from the tail of the dog that bit you on the wound – both bizarre and barking!

# HAIR RAISING

'They're not grey hairs. They're wisdom highlights.'

UNKNOWN

'He doesn't dye his hair. He's just prematurely orange.'

GERALD FORD, SPEAKING ABOUT RONALD REAGAN

'I'm not offended by all the dumb-blonde jokes because I know that I'm not dumb. I also know I'm not blonde.'

DOLLY PARTON

'The solution to a bad hair day is to wear a low-cut blouse.'

UNKNOWN

'Grey hair is a blessing – ask any bald man.'

UNKNOWN

# How to Keep Granny Sweet

When things are getting a little fraught, your nerves are on edge and you're beginning to climb the walls – at least, you would if you could – leave your copy of *Granny Knows Best* open at this page and little eyes (or those of their parents) might just read some of these hints on how not to annoy Granny. You deserve some me-time too. Some 'Gran-me' time. So, dear grandchild (and parents), here's how to keep Granny sweet:

To whom it may concern:

## 1. TIME OUT
It doesn't have to be too long – half an hour is fine – but letting me have a quiet cup of coffee or tea, a chance to check my emails and powder my nose is IMPORTANT. Being a grandma may be a full-time job, but breaks are required by law for most workers so why not for grannies too? Peace and quiet are among the greatest gifts you can give me ... if only for ten minutes.

## 2. APPRECIATION
Homemade cards, thank-you notes, a hand-picked posy from the garden, or other little, inexpensive signs of gratitude are worth far more to most grannies than big, flashy, shop-bought gifts. I love you and I know you love me, but it's always nice to know that my kindness and hard work (I won't mention all those hours of unpaid child-minding) are not being taken for granted. You are my world, but I do have other things to do sometimes: bake for the village fête, read (or write) a novel, learn the tango for ballroom dancing class, go to work/on a date/to Bermuda ...

### 3. BE GOOD

Respect and good behaviour go hand in hand and both are appreciated by grannies. If you're out with Granny, being good is the best thing to be. No tantrums, no whingeing, no running off, no hiding in supermarkets. Nobody gets upset, rewards may be forthcoming – it's a win-win situation. That's how to win over Granny!

### 4. START SCHOOL.

# *Keeping Busy*

**The devil makes work for idle hands. And what's more, they are the devil's playthings. This applies to hands of all sizes and genders, including Grandpa's in some cases. It might even apply to yours on occasion, although they are probably full of work, tasks, chores and projects for at least 364 days a year.**

Small hands, however, are another matter. Small idle hands are at their most dangerous when covered in unidentifiable sticky substances or armed with things that stain, chip or streak at will – things that are innocent everyday items in the hands of an adult, but lethal weapons in the hands of a toddler.

Medium-sized hands can be just as annoying and perilous to one's well-being if glued to a device of some kind without interruption, except to receive food and drink, adjust headphones or answer a smartphone.

Large grandpa-shaped hands can be encouraged into the kitchen, garden, allotment, garage, supermarket, shed, car or next town to perform useful tasks and return with the fruits of their labour, caveman-style. You could even do some of the chores together to avoid chore wars. Teamwork makes the dream work, as they say, but when you are in charge of the grandchildren, organisation is required.

## All hands to the pump.

*There's nothing like teamwork (and sometimes in your household there is nothing like teamwork).*

## An idle brain is the devil's workshop.

*That devil chap is a bit of a workaholic.*

## A lazy sheep thinks its wool heavy.

*Like some teenagers and their homework.*

## Whatever you're doing, stop it at once.

*A catch-all for when you are really pushed …*

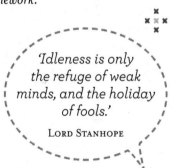

*'Idleness is only the refuge of weak minds, and the holiday of fools.'*

LORD STANHOPE

## All work and no play makes Jack a dull boy.

*But all play and no work makes having Jack a dull joy.*

## Beat boredom with choredom.

*Author of this useful threat unknown.*


## Many hands make the lights work.

*And other variations by Mrs Malaprop.*


## Some are always busy and never do anything.

*There's a difference between being busy and being productive.*


## Ask not what your granny can do for you, but what you can do for your granny.

*This should be on a poster!*

## KEEPING THE GRANDKIDS BUSY

You may not remember having either the time or the opportunity to be bored 'in your day' (see Don'ts, page 74), but 'I'm bored' seems to be the mantra and complaint of the young. Giving them a task – and indeed the same task – each time they visit is a good idea. It establishes roles, routine and responsibility. And it helps you and keeps them away from screens, fridges and biscuit tins (the three wicked witches of boredom).

For younger children, a supply of paper, paints and crayons, plus stocks of cardboard, craft glue, scissors and tin foil (surprisingly useful) are important. Keep old magazines, scraps of fabric and cardboard boxes for collage purposes. Suggest making up memory boxes, sewing clothes, baking cakes for charity. Try to get them to think outside the (X-)box.

Visit places to stimulate their imagination or encourage future interests and career choices: local farms, zoos, markets, bookshops, galleries, your office. Send the older grandchildren computer links to interesting articles or interviews, or subscriptions to magazines.

Watch old films that inspired you, tell them about books you love, personalities you admire, talk to them about yourself and what you did when you were their age. Try to introduce them to new ideas. Staying one step ahead of them will keep a spring in yours.

# THE BUSINESS OF BUSYNESS

'People say nothing
is impossible, but I do
nothing every day.'

WINNIE-THE-POOH

'If you want work
well done, select a
busy man, the other
kind has no time.'

ELBERT HUBBARD — HE
COULD HAVE SAID THE
SAME FOR A WOMAN!

'The happiest part of a man's
life is what he passes lying
awake in bed in the morning.'

SAMUEL JOHNSON

'A teacher's purpose is not to create students in his own image, but to develop students who can create their own image.'

UNKNOWN

'For Kim did nothing with an immense success.'

RUDYARD KIPLING

'When you teach your son, you teach your son's son.'

THE TALMUD (So when you teach your son's son, you are teaching your son's son's son, too.)

'Idleness is fatal only to the mediocre.'

ALBERT CAMUS

Granny
Wisdom

# Beautifying Yourself

**Women have always wanted to look good and today there's a billion-pound industry that invests millions on advertising, with the specific aim of getting you to part with your hard-earned money or pension to roll back the years or keep the wrinkles at bay.**

But grannies know a thing or two about natural beauty products, often learned from their mothers who did not have the benefit (?) of today's huge cosmetics industry. After all, could Cleopatra (or indeed, Tutankhamun) pop down to the local chemist for their kohl eyeliner? Did Boudica get a delivery of waterproof mascara before advancing on her enemies? Did Marie-Antoinette send out flunkies to scour the shelves for a cleansing face mask, beauty spots and a big-hair wig? There are many homemade treatments to try at a fraction of the cost of the big industry names – all you have to do is open the store cupboard. And never underestimate the value of soap and water and a good night's sleep. And all this because you're worth it! Here is a handy guide of beauty tips to hand down to the next generation.

## AN EGG ON YOUR FACE

Fancy a rejuvenating face mask? Whisk 1 egg white together with 1 teaspoon of lemon juice until frothy. Stir in half a teaspoon of runny honey. Apply to your face, avoiding mouth and eyes, and relax with a magazine for 10 to 15 minutes. Then gently wash off the mask with warm water and pat your face dry.

## EYES TO THE RIGHT

To help get rid of an unsightly panda look (those dark circles under your eyes), try mixing 1 teaspoon of tomato juice with ½–1 teaspoon of lemon juice and placing it under your eyes. Leave to dry for 10 minutes and then wash off gently with water and pat dry. Don't let any of it get in your eyes – it will sting like hell.

## EYES BRIGHT

Cool and fresh cucumber slices applied to the eyes for 5 to 10 minutes work on many levels: they keep a granddaughter quiet if you do it together and reduce puffiness (possibly

> 'All the carnal beauty of my wife is but skin deep.'
> SIR THOMAS OVERBURY

caused by the aforementioned). The antioxidants help with irritation and their coolness reduces swelling. An unpeeled cucumber can help rub crayon marks off the wall too. Result!

## OAT SO BEAUTIFUL

For an oatmeal face mask, mix together ½ cup of oatmeal (preferably ground down to a powder) with ¼ cup of water, and stir in 2 teaspoons of runny honey. Then proceed as above.

## RAPUNZEL

Do you wake up with your hair in a tangle? Changing your cotton pillowcase for a silk or satin one should fix that and may even reduce wrinkles too – anything that helps!

Having followed your own advice, your grandchildren will no longer recognise you. 'You look different, Granny! Have you had Botox?' So now is the time to dispense a few wise words on beauty – which, as we all know, is in the eye of the beholder.

## A bonnie face needs nae band.

*Don't overdo the make-up or the bling.*

## Don't gild the lily.

*Ditto but without the Scottish accent.*

## Beauty may have fair leaves yet bitter fruit.

*It's not all it is cracked up to be.*

## Beauty is only skin-deep, but ugly goes straight to the bone.

*Ouch.*

## All that glitters is not gold.

*But it looks good on the dance floor.*

## Age before beauty.

*Not as far as you're concerned.*

## Beauty opens locked doors.

*But an attractive personality counts for a lot, too.*

## Beauty is a good letter of introduction.

*But the meeting of minds is better.*

## Prettiness makes no pottage.

*A warning to swains of yore whose heads might have been turned by a pretty ankle. In other words, choose a plain wife if you want to eat well. Cheek!*

# THE BEAUTY OF WORDS

The first two quotes have
become so popular they
have become proverbs.

'A thing of
beauty is a joy
forever.'

JOHN KEATS

'The face
that launch'd
a thousand
ships.'

CHRISTOPHER
MARLOWE

'It is better to be
beautiful than to be good,
but it is better to be good
than to be ugly.'

OSCAR WILDE

'We find delight in the beauty and happiness of children that makes the heart too big for the body.'

RALPH WALDO EMERSON

'Beauty awakens the soul to act.'

DANTE

'Beauty and folly are old companions.'

BENJAMIN FRANKLIN

'Shall I compare thee to a summer's day? Thou art more lovely and more temperate.'

WILLIAM SHAKESPEARE

# How to Be a Glam-ma

Calling all glam-orous ma-triarchs, all gorgeous ladies and mothers of mothers and fathers (Glamms and Glammfs – an interesting acronym, it might catch on) – it may be time to ditch the rocking chair, the boiled sweets and the flowery apron. Here's how to give the Glam-grans in the magazines a run (or at least a brisk walk) for their money. Glam-ma is the new Grandma.

## RECLAIM YOUR IDENTITY

You are you. You might be a mother/grandmother – but you are also far more than that. Don't fade into the background. Some mothers and grandmothers feel they can't be themselves. Let your individual style loose now. Wear that bright nail varnish. Try that lipstick. Get those boots. Buy that bag you always wanted. Treat yourself to a trip to that expensive new hair salon. You don't have to go grey until you're ready to do so.

## DON'T BE INVISIBLE

Invest in some stylish sunglasses and a statement capsule wardrobe. Don't be invisible. You don't have to wear granny camouflage. Stand out. Invest in you. Put the sensible shoes, the cardigan and the skirt that will 'see you out' at the back of the wardrobe.

## TAKE UP NEW HOBBIES

Line dancing, poker, life drawing – in fact why not be a life drawing model! Join a book, baking, bingo or bridge club.

## GO TRAVELLING

Not over the hill, but up mountains, down rivers, on safari ...

## A ROSE BY ANY OTHER NAME

And finally, forbid the grandkids from shouting 'Grandma, hurry up!' when you're out in public. Get them to call you by your first name – people will assume you're an aunt/older mother/au pair – or decide to be foreign and exotic and choose one of the alternatives from the international selection on page 128.

Granny
Wisdom

# Keeping Sprightly

**Grannies today are hip, not hip operation. And some grannies are more hip-hop than hip-op.**

Get on that dance floor, Glam-ma, and strut your stuff, or at least shake a leg. You can save a few Bob by dumping Jim but keep using Shanks's pony, as the new saying goes. And to quote an old one, *mens sana in corpore sano* ('a sound mind in a sound body' – the two go hand in hand), so it's good to keep your mind active, too. But if you impart any of the following get-fit wit and wisdom without practising what you preach, your grandkids or sneering peers will soon let you know about it. So keep the gin and the chocolate well hidden and leave your gym membership card lying around casually for all to see, even if it has expired.

## After dinner sit awhile, after supper walk a mile.

*Don't rush out for a jog after dinner, wait until after supper.*

## An apple a day keeps the doctor away.

*Tell that to Little Red Riding Hood and Snow White.*

## If they would drink nettles in March, and eat mugwort in May, so many fine maidens wouldn't go to the clay.

*Would you like to supersize/take fries with that? Wise words for maidens addicted to fast food.*

## You are what you eat.

*Don't say this to a teenage girl about to have a bacon butty.*

## A little of what you fancy does you good.

*Only a little? Really? Surely that should be 'a vast vat/tub of'.*

## After cheese comes nothing.

*Tell that to the French. After cheese come the just desserts.*

## It's better to eat to live and not live to eat.

*Whoever likes to quote this clearly has never tasted hot chocolate fudge cake, banoffee pie, treacle tart, peanut butter and chocolate chip cheesecake.*

# FIT BITS

'Wine is the most healthful and most hygienic of beverages.'

LOUIS PASTEUR

'I have to exercise in the morning before my brain finds out what I'm doing.'

MARSHA DOBLE

'Drink tea and nourish life. With the first sip, joy. With the second, satisfaction. With the third, peace. With the fourth, a Danish.'

UNKNOWN

'The trouble with jogging is that by the time you realise you're not in shape for it, it's too far to walk back.'

FRANKLIN JONES